Prison

Book 5

True Diary Entries
by a Maximum-Security Prison Officer

October, 2018

Copyright © 2019 by Simon King

All rights reserved. This book or any portion thereof may not be reproduced or used in any manner whatsoever without the express written permission of the publisher except for the use of brief quotations in a book review or scholarly journal.
First Printing: 2019

By Simon King

Prison Days June

Prison Days July

Prison Days August

Prison Days September

Prison Days- The First Four Months

COMING SOON

Prison Days November (December 1ˢᵗ)

The Final Alibi

Introduction

It is a Saturday night, or should I say Sunday morning, 12:57 in the morning to be precise; and the unit is echoing with the endless screaming of prisoners continuously "burning" each other. It's just another shift for me, sitting alone in the officer's station of the hardest unit in the prison. Is it fun? No. Is it exciting? No. It's mind-numbing as I listen to the constant bantering of first one lot of prisoners yelling abuse at each other, followed by the other group. The intercom kicks in occasionally as individual prisoners buzz me, asking how much longer the yelling is going to continue. I tell them that I don't know. Some nights it stops around 10, other nights at 11. Some nights it begins to fade around 1. Tonight, seems to be one of the late ones where no-one wants to sleep. It's cold, almost freezing in fact.

Personally, I just want to tell them all to shut the fuck up, but I know I can't. I am nothing more than a passenger, forced to listen and monitor. I've turned the unit lights off and I'm hoping that they might get the hint but the longer I sit here with the voices continuing to roar, hope quickly fades to despair. This is what Maximum is all about. It's not about going toe to toe; seeing who can yell the loudest. For us officers, it's about knowing when to speak and when to shut up. Having the prisoners burn each other is actually a good thing; as long as they are abusing each other, they aren't abusing me, and that's a win. It means they leave me alone and I can sit here and talk to you instead.

I'm in awe at the realisation that this edition marks the fifth outing. It's already been five books and there is still so much to share. This month has been another crazy journey through the darkness that is life behind bars. Several prisoners have been stabbed; plenty of assaults; one prisoner that thought he was ready to die while another was mistaken for Superman. There's so much to get through and I know you can't wait to read about it. If you do like my war stories, then please don't forget to leave a review. Books without them really do fade into the vast abyss that exists on the internet.

Now, hang on tight as I unlock the door, and follow me inside. Please try and stay close, there are teeth behind these walls; teeth that bite.

Units

All the units in the prison are named after rivers and consist of management, step-down management, protection and main stream.

Management Units

Units that are predominately single occupancy out of necessity or punishment and have 23-hour lock ins. Prisoners only receive a one hour run out from their cell.
Murray North and South are the Management Units.

Step Down Management

Units that are a step down from the 23-hour lock down. Prisoners are given extra run-outs throughout the day but limited to around 3 to 4 hours. Some prisoners can mix and have joint run-outs.
Goulburn East and West are the Step-Down Management Units.

Protection Units

Yarra North and South, Loddon North and South, Glenelg East and West

Main Stream Units

Thomson East and West, Tambo East and West, Campaspe, Avoca, Maribyrnong,

Other Areas

Kitchen, Laundry, Medical Wing, Reception

Some Prison Terms

- Air- Raiding- Yelling or abusing someone loudly in the middle of a unit.

- Billet- A prisoner who is assigned a particular duty in the unit, on a daily basis, for a weekly pay packet. They hold the position until they are either transferred out, sacked or quit.

- Bone Yard- A protection unit. Protection prisoners are also known as Boners.

- Booted- To hide something in the anus

- Boss- What prisoners call an officer. It began early last century, is a reverse insult and means "Sorry Son of a Bitch"

- Brew- A cup of Coffee or Tea

- Brasco- Toilet or brasco roll is toilet paper.

- Bronze Up- To cover ones' self in faeces.

- Bunk- A prisoner's bed.

- Burning- Prisoners abusing a crook or officer for an extended period of time.

- Canteen- A prisoner's weekly shopping or shopping items.

- Cellie- A cellmate

- Chook Pen- A fenced-in area attached to a unit for prisoners to walk around in. Approximately 15m by 15m depending on which unit. Management units have multiple chook pens as prisoners have individual run outs throughout the day.

- Co-ee- A prisoner's co-accused

- Crook- How officers refer to inmates

- Dog- Someone who informs on another prisoner.
- Greens or Greys- Prisoner's prison uniform.
- Rock Spider- A paedophile.
- Screw- How inmates refer to officers.
- Shiv- home-made knife or blade.
- Slash Up- To self-harm
- The T.O.'s- Tactical Officers, that are highly trained and armed with batons and O.C. spray.
- Trap- A small latch in a cell door that can be lowered to allow access. It is normally either half way up or three quarters of the way up the cell door.

Codes

- Alpha- Officer needs assistance, Officer emergency
- Bravo- Lock down of Unit
- Charlie- Lock down of prison
- Delta- Fire
- Echo- Escape
- Foxtrot- Fight, Prisoner on Prisoner
- Mike- Medical emergency

Monday, October 1

It's the first day of a new month and I'm relatively happy as I walk in through reception. I'm greeted by the Reception staff and proceed to be scanned and checked. I see my friend Kon a few spots ahead of me and call out to him. He turns to me and flashes his big Greek grin at me.

"Where are you today?" he asks as I finish grabbing my bag and follow him into the key room. It is a controlled airlock with only half a dozen officers allowed entry at any one time. It's quite a tight space and we form a line in front of the thick glass window; it reminds me of a bank teller, one Control Room officer frantically grabbing radios and keys for each officer as they front the queue. Most mornings, the process can be quite frustrating and takes a lot of patience. There are more than a hundred staff that start at the same time and every one of them requires a personal radio and a set of keys. Each set of keys has already been allocated to an officer by the Control Room night staff but mistakes can and do happen and when they do, slows the process down considerably.

The prison also operates some doors with swipe cards and these have an active life of 12 months. Once the expiry date passes, your card is ineffective when attempting to move through certain doors. As I swipe mine, the little light remains red instead of blinking green.

"I'm in Glenelg West," I replied, retrying my card a second time, knowing full well what the problem was.

"So am I," Kon said as he fronts the line and grabs his gear.

"I'll have to catch up with you, card not working." He gives me a thumbs up and shuffles through the other door, leaving me to wait for my card to be reactivated, once I have my keys and radio.

It's a good 20 minutes before I'm finally in the unit, briefly stopping for a chat with Thelma who was on night shift. We pass each other in one of the corridors and she waves me down.

"Good night?" I ask and her frown is immediate.

"Shit. Fucken goose kept bangin up all night. The other crooks gave him quite a burning and he reciprocated by keeping them awake all night. Didn't quieten till almost 4. Where are you today?"

"Glenelg West," I tell her.

"Well, you should have a fun day. They took Robert Bester there earlier this morning. He was one of the Code Foxtrot's from last night. Got smacked around a bit and they took him out for a check-up." Sometimes, prisoners will be shuttled out by ambulance and taken to a nearby hospital for precautionary exams. It depends on the severity but if a prisoner is suspected of having internal injuries then prison medical staff won't take the chance, instead sending the crook out for a more in-depth examination. Unfortunately, prisoners know this and will often, way too often, fake injuries or conditions to either bail out of a unit or simply waste resources. It means nothing to them to tie up an ambulance for several hours by faking a heart attack.

"Great, can't wait. You have a good sleep," I say and we part ways, Thelma heading out while I head in, each of us on opposite ends of the merry-go-round.

I can hear a dull thumping sound as I come through the airlock, Kon standing in the officer's station with Scott Jones. I wave and go and stow my things before returning to the station, the banging continuing with a slow methodical continuity.

"Bester?" I ask as I shake hands with Scott and he nods.

"I got here half hour ago and he was going at it then." A couple of prisoners yell for him to shut the fuck up but he continues, despite the protests from others. I check the muster sheet and get a brief idea of who was in the unit. Being mostly long-term protection meant the main bulk of the unit's population were older sex offenders. There were a couple of young hotheads thrown in for good measure, but overall, it was a fairly quiet unit.

But a unit's atmosphere can change and sometimes the changes can be quite dramatic depending on who is brought in and who is shifted out. Units can go from being classed as "retirement villages" for the staff working there to "Bronx Status" in a matter of a few days. In recent weeks, Glenelg West has been relatively quiet; not quite a retirement home but close enough.

Control calls for count and Kon and I begin the morning round. I grab the muster and mark the cells off as Kon drops the traps, peers inside and confirms each cell's occupancy. We leave the first cell on the bottom tier for last, its sole occupant continuing to beat his war drums.

The trip around the unit is over in just under 10 minutes and as a precaution, we double check on Robert to ensure he's OK. His cell is an observation cell which comes with the added bonus of an in-built camera. Every unit has 3 observation cells, usually reserved for prisoners that are on suicide watch. One of the first things most non-compliant prisoners do is cover the camera with wet toilet paper. Some will do it only as a privacy measure while they take care of their toilet needs, uncovering the camera once finished. But for others, they see it as another opportunity to thumb their nose at any form of authority, often using the camera as a bargaining tool.

Observation cells have two doors, one being the inner door which is a very thick and transparent Perspex, steel bars running across its width in short intervals. The outer door, known as the "outer skin" is thinner than most of the steel doors but still reinforced metal. The outer skin can be safely opened, leaving the inner door secure. Kon unlocks Robert's outer skin door and we peer in at him. He's lying on his back with his eyes closed and one arm over his face. He has his feet planted on the door and stomps each of them in regular intervals of about five or so seconds. He doesn't hear us open the door and Kon kicks the door to get his attention. He opens his eyes and jumps to his feet when he sees us.

"What the fuck you want?" he screams then punches the door. Seeing him move OK, we close the outer skin as he lands another punch, the bang echoing through my brain. It's followed by a kick and then a barrage of punches.

Robert Bester's brain is what you would call fried. Too many date nights with crystal meth has seen him become an almost mumbling psycho that can bounce through emotional states like an earthquake up the Richter scale. He can go from happy to sad to pure rage within a minute. He is extremely volatile and highly unpredictable and that makes him quite dangerous.

We return to the station and add up our numbers, calling them in once finished. It's not long before they call count correct and Scott and I head out and unlock the cells. Within minutes, the unit is a hive of activity as crooks begin their normal routines. Several come to the station and vent their grievances at the new tenant. They know we can't change his allocation to the unit and thus simply use us to vent. It's not something we try and avoid as a good venting now can prevent a blow-up down the line.

The morning runs smoothly as the medication trolley enters the unit and the meds are all handed out quietly with minimum fuss. Robert also requires meds but when we drop the trap for the nurse to give them, he tries to spit at us. He misses and I slam the trap back in place as he restarts his door kicking. The nurse is happy for him to miss out and we move on with our day.

There are 3 prisoners that are leaving the unit today and we inform them to pack their gear. Once they are ready, a fourth officer comes to escort them to Admissions. There are two new arrivals later in the day but after reshuffling a bit, we find a spare single cell available. Several of the prisoners are also aware of the vacancy and don't delay in trying to secure it for themselves. But they know there's a list of offering and once we check it, notify the proud new tenant who happily runs off to move into his new home.

Lunchtime count is called just as I check which cells are up for searching today and I set the list aside, grabbing the muster sheet while Scott announces muster over the unit P.A. system. The prisoners begin to line up and we begin the task of counting the unit. Halfway through, there's a loud crashing from Robert's cell. We ignore it as we focus on count, knowing that it takes priority. When I reach Robert's cell, I open the outer door and watch as he is kicking the metal toilet. I close it again and head for the station to tally up the numbers.

Control calls count correct a few minutes after we call our number through and Kon leads Scott around for the cell searches. The kicking from Robert's cell continues as I begin to adjust the unit muster on the computer, moving departures out and new cell allocations in. Half an hour later the boys return from their searching empty handed. Just as Kon is about to say something, Scott groans.

"He's flooding up," he said, pointing towards Robert's cell. I look and see water running out from under the door. I follow the other two as we head to the cell. Kon opens the skin and drops the trap. Robert is in the process of tearing his mattress apart. Water is shooting from the shower head and the foam from the mattress has clogged the drain.

 "Robert!" Kon shouts. No response. "ROBERT!" Kon shouts again and also kicks the door. Robert stops and looks at us, a fire burning in his eyes. "Need you to turn the shower off, man," Kon said but Robert shakes his head.

"I can't."

"Robert, I need the shower turned off. It's flooding the unit. Otherwise I'll have to shut the water off."

"I can't," Robert repeats and when we take a closer look, see the issue. Robert is correct when he says he's unable to turn the shower off. He has managed to tear the shower, including the metal water pipe, completely out of the wall, bits of cement dotted around his floor. He has also managed to tear the sink from the wall and his toilet is sitting at a skewed angle. The strength needed to do the damage that he's caused in that little time is incredible.

Scott immediately calls the Supervisor on the radio and asks her to attend the unit as Robert restarts his assault on the door. The Supervisor enters a few minutes later and immediately opens the water cabinet which sits next to the cell door. The water is shut off and she attempts to talk to Robert through the door. He refuses, continuing to kick the inner door. Eventually she gives up and calls for the Tactical boys to attend. She then calls Murray North and asks them to prepare one of their cells. The rest of us lock the unit down, much to the complaints of the other prisoners. They enjoy a good show but, in this case, we need the unit empty and thus they miss out. The main reason is that as Robert has been quite a pain already, one of the other prisoners may choose to shit-bomb him on the way out.

Unfortunately, he does require running water and a working toilet, and although he may do the same to his new cell, we have no choice but to have him moved. Four tactical boys turn up ten minutes later and prepare to extract him. They prep a large shield as the Supervisor once again attempts to talk him down. His reply is a barrage of spit and abuse and when the Supervisor steps aside, waves her hands like a quiz show prize presenter.

"All yours, boys," she says and walks to the station. One of the boys, dressed in riot helmet and protective suit, walks to the trap.

"Last chance, Robert," he says but Robert stands with his fists at the ready. The officer nods his head and raises the shield, two others lining up behind him and grabbing the protection suit handles that sit on the back of the suit. They will turn into a human train, propelled by three sets of legs, the shield held before them like a battering ram. The fourth officer opens the inner door quickly and the three boys charge past him with grunts of effort. The shield first slams into Robert's fists, then into his torso as his arms crumple at the force of the approaching wall. His legs try and brace him but only for a split second. He is body-slammed almost instantly into the wall behind him, his legs becoming tangled as he falls to the ground. The third officer reaches around and grabs one wrist, pulling it out and down. The second officer pulls his other wrist out and down, pinning his top half down onto the wet concrete floor. The first officer throws the shield to the side and lands on Robert's ankles, pinning his legs as the fourth officer now enters with handcuffs in hand. Robert is screaming every profanity imaginable, struggling hard against his captors as his breathing becomes short and laboured puffs of rage.

Once his hands are securely cuffed, a spit mask is put over his head to prevent him shooting saliva at officers. Then, they pick him up, one on either side of him. While Robert is facing the rear of the cell, the officers face the front, each with an arm through the loops of Robert's arms. When they begin walking Robert out backwards, he's taken off balance, making it extremely difficult for him to struggle as the officer's arms interlock together like a weight-bearing pole carrying a pig carcass off to a bonfire. Robert has no choice but to follow. The unit erupts with cheers and whistles as he is led out through the airlock and I'm thankful to see the back of him.

We unlock the unit shortly after and after answering a few questions from curious prisoners, relax into a quiet afternoon. It has been a pretty interesting day and although one cell was completely destroyed, no officers were hurt. A couple of new arrivals turn up shortly after and are allocated their new cells. The unit billet shows them around as we watch the afternoon unfold. As we walk out a few hours later, I shake my offsider's hands. We are all back together tomorrow, to do it all again.

Today has been a good day.

Tuesday, October 2

Came in expecting to return to Glenelg West but halfway to the unit was asked to do some urine testing instead. It's one of those jobs that a lot of people frown about. Me? I don't mind it. It means you can conduct your day freely without having to sit still in a unit station. Plus, there's the added bonus of not having fifty crooks in your face nonstop throughout the day.

Miguel Foster and Chris Upton, two officers I hadn't seen in a while were already in the urinalysis room when I walked in. They were a couple of funny guys to work with and I knew the day would pass without too much pain; prisoners aside of course.

"Going to the funeral on Thursday?" Chris asked and I nodded (see September Edition).

"Wouldn't miss it," I said. He handed me the daily list and I ran my eyes across it, looking for any familiar names that would give us grief. I couldn't see any and handed it back.

We waited until Control called the morning count correct and Chris phoned the first unit for a couple of mainstreamers to come up. It doesn't take long for them to show which is a good thing for us as it means they are keen to get things over with. One we lock in a holding cell then escort the other to the sample room. Sometimes things just tend to 'flow' smoothly, pardon the pun, and this morning happens to be one of those days. Each lot of prisoners are processed within minutes of arriving and head back out the door a short time later. I know it doesn't make for interesting reading for you, but for us it really is a relief.

By the time lunchtime count is called for, our list of 28 is reduced to just 12, the majority already tagged and bagged. The remaining names on the list are Protection prisoners and Miguel and Chris head out to the first unit once count is correct, while I wait behind and prepare the room, ensuring our supplies are all sufficiently stocked. Nothing worse than having a fresh cup of piss and no tape with which to seal it.

The boys return with 4 prisoners in tow and all of them ask for water and time. Chris and I exchange a look that needs no words; protection. I don't know what the reason is but protection prisoners are simply so much more difficult to deal with, both in a unit and out of it. They have an air of need about them, constantly in officer's ears about things they require urgently, as in right now. They have a habit of being in your face for the entire day, complain so much more, require physical escorts whenever they leave the unit and think they are so much more important than regular crooks.

It's almost half an hour before we hear the faint tap from one of the prisoners who's ready to piss. I open the door, usher him out and lead him into the sample room where Chris conducts a full strip, looking for anything that might be used to adulterate the sample. He checks out and once he's half-dressed himself again, grabs a sample jar.

Now, every prisoner that I have ever piss tested, despite some strange methods for warming their dick up, has performed the task as you would normally expect; standing before the bowl and waiting for the stream to begin and then catching the urine in the jar. Imagine my surprise when Jake Bauer takes the jar, spins around and then promptly sits on the toilet with his hand between his legs. When he sees me looking at him curiously, he offers a slight smile.

"I don't urinate standing like some ape," he said as I heard the trickle begin.

"Whatever works, man," I replied, Chris chuckling next to me. After a few seconds, the crook stands, flushes, then pours half his sample into a second jar before sealing both jars and then handing them to me for processing. I seal the lids with security tape and then place them in separate plastic bags which I also seal with tape. The prisoner signs both lots of tape to ensure there's no issues down the track. We prepare two separate samples so that if there's an issue with the first one, the prisoner can elect to have the second sample tested.

"You're all done," Chris tells him and we lock him into a separate cell while Miguel calls for his transport back to the unit. I know it's quite normal for some men to squat while urinating. I've just never seen it done while providing a sample.

Another crook begins tapping on his cell door and when Chris escorts him in, I can tell immediately that he's hiding something. Some prisoner's just have a certain look on their faces when they're up to no good. It's like a smirk that they can't seem to hide. As Chris begins to conduct the strip search, I inspect each piece of clothing but find nothing as Chris continues to talk the prisoner through the process.

Once he finishes the inspection of his private bits, Chris motions for the prisoner to take a sample jar and commence the test. He grabs the jar then turns his back to us and faces the toilet bowl. Chris and I look at each other, knowing that he's up to something even before he begins the routine. I step slightly to my right to try and get a better look from the prisoner's side while Chris watches the convex mirror that is hanging on the wall above the toilet. It allows us to see the prisoner front on but due to the distance and distortion, can prove to be less than helpful at times.

The prisoner stands still, one hand holding the jar under his dick, the other on his hip. He begins scratching his head, then nose. Chris motions for me to look and I step forward a little.

"All good, man?" I ask and the prisoner looks at me.

"Give me a minute. It's coming," he replies then turns his head slightly away. He yawns, covering his mouth with one hand. His hand remains at his mouth and then he yawns again. Chris looks at me, holding his hands up questioningly. 'What's he doing' he mouths to me and I shrug my shoulders, unable to see. His hand is still on his mouth and without warning, makes a retching noise. He bends slightly forward, makes another retching noise, then leans forward and vomits into the bowl as his face turns a crimson red, spluttering as he drops the sample jar. I can see something dangling between his mouth and the toilet bowl and as he tries to reach for it, misses as he vomits a second time. I step forward and before he has a chance to regain his composure, reach in and grab whatever is floating in mid-air.

It's a finger from a rubber glove, tied to a piece of dental floss that's still attached to the crook's dental braces. Chris and I stare at it in total disbelief as the prisoner is still trying to get his stomach under control. He looks at the rubber finger wide-eyed, not because we have it but because it's empty, a small hole sitting just below the tie-off point. Chris erupts into laughter as the prisoner continues retching.

"Hope your donor was a close friend, dude," I said, fighting my own laughter. The prisoner was white as a sheet as we held out the sample jar to him.

"Care to provide a proper sample?" Chris asked but he shook his head. We escorted him to another cell, then contacted the duty Sup. It was a very good reminder that in prison, there's no such thing as "seen it all before".

The prisoner was eventually charged with attempting to adulterate a sample and was given a fine. We continued our day and finished the piss testing with no other exciting stories.

Chris and I laughed as we walked out the gate a couple of hours later, still bemused at the poor bloke's misjudgement of gargling his mate's piss.

Today was a good day.

Wednesday, October 3

Today, I was rostered in Thomson East and although some days can feel like they are going as smooth as one could wish for, things can change at any moment in the blink of an eye. In fact, the whole day can run according to schedule and just as you slam home that final door, sure that you're about to drop the curtain on another incident-free day, the proverbial shit can hit the fan. That's what happened today.

The whole day had gone by with relative calmness, the bulk of the prisoners playing nicely together. Myself, Thelma and Robert Nixon, both of my offsiders very experienced officers, had enjoyed a drama-free day from beginning to end without so much as a single incident. Not even a hat worn inside the unit. It was as if everyone just had one of those days where they couldn't be stuffed doing anything other than what was needed.

The medication runs had come and gone with nothing to note; the random cell searches were completed with all crooks willingly opening their doors for us and leaving us to our searches; each muster had come and gone with such quietness that I believed we could have heard a pin drop. Like I said, the day was a non-event as far as we were concerned. Good for us, but unfortunately not so good for you reading this for a bit of excitement.

The afternoon went by with us officers watching a very animated poker match where half a dozen prisoners were playing for a substantial pot which included several bottles of Coke, several large blocks of chocolate and half a dozen bags of crisps. There were also about a dozen Mars bars and one lonely packet of 2-minute noodles.

The final hand was finished just as the 5 o'clock muster was called and the winner hurriedly carted his winnings to his cell, much to the delight of his cell mate who was already eyeing off the chocolate. He kept trying to help his cellie with carrying the goods but had his hand slapped away several times, much to the amusement of the rest of the unit.

Dinner was served on time and with very little fanfare. It was Chicken Maryland for those interested, served with gravy and mashed potato. A chocolate chip cookie finished the meal and once final count was called, the prisoners headed back to their cell doors, patiently waiting as we came around to conduct the final count and subsequently lock them in.

Once all the doors were locked, we all headed back to the station and tallied our counts. Once we confirmed our numbers matched, it was just a matter of waiting until count was called correct and we'd be free to leave. Count was indeed called correct a few minutes later and we grabbed our bags to leave. Thelma was holding the door open as Robert walked into the airlock, both waiting for me to turn the computer off. Just as I grabbed my bag and walked down the couple of stairs out of the station, I heard something. It sounded like a sharp whip crack, followed by the faintest yelp. I stopped, paused and looked into the unit. It was silent again and as I stood, heard Thelma call out to me. I was about to answer her, when I heard another sound, and this time I recognized it for what it was. It sounded like a slap, followed by a low grunt. I dropped my bag and gestured to my offsiders. They came back into the unit and we spread out to try and locate the source of the sounds.

"Here," Robert finally said as he approached a cell on the bottom tier. As I ran over, he opened the trap and peered in. It was the cell of the winner of the poker game and as I approached, had a good idea of what the issue would be.

"Code Foxtrot, Thomson East," Thelma called into her radio as Robert began yelling at the prisoners inside the cell. I tried to look past him, over his shoulder, but the small trap made it almost impossible. As Robert turned his head to say something to Thelma, I saw what he'd been trying to stop. Adrian Kemp, the winner of the Poker game, had his much smaller cellmate, David Bruce, by the scruff and was pushing him against the window. David had been pushed up far enough that his buttocks were sitting on the window ledge. His face looked completely pulverized, both eyes purple and closed. He looked unconscious as Adrian continued to punch David in the face, each time the fist connecting with him, the back of his head would bang against the window. Adrian sounded out of breath yet continued to punch again and again and again.

"Urgent medical care needed. Permission to open cell," Thelma yelled into her radio. Once the cells had been locked and the final count called correct, any opening of cells had to be authorized, regardless of the reason. Thankfully for us, the night Sup was listening and gave us the OK. Robert cracked the door and both of us rushed in, grabbing Adrian's arms as a limp David slumped onto the floor.

"I ain't resisting. Thieving cunt had it comin to him," Adrian said as I cuffed his hands. We walked him out of the cell as Thelma tended to David. I turned to see her place the unconscious prisoner into a recovery position as the first officers burst through the air lock and into the unit.

As we lead Adrian out of the unit, a couple of other prisoners begin yelling but the doors close before I could tell whether they were Supporting Adrian or condemning him. If his statement was true, that David was a thief, then the prisoners would more than likely support him. Thieving is a definite no-no in prison and as I've just described, can be dealt with swiftly and usually with severe consequences. Even in a unit filled with thieves, thieving is never accepted.

Robert and I are greeted by the Tactical Officers who take Adrian and escort him to the Admissions area. He'll face a lengthy wait as the Police will be called out to investigate the crime scene as well as conduct their interviews. Robert and I return to the unit and begin to write our reports alongside Thelma who is in the middle of her own, just as a stretcher arrives. David is lifted onto it and wheeled briskly from the unit to more chants of "maggot", "dog" and "grub".

Once our reports are finished and handed to the Supervisor, we are free to head home, our job finally complete. Although the day was a good one, it really didn't end well.

Thursday, October 4

The funeral of Robert Hall (see September edition). Sometimes, there are days that really impact on one's conscience, in more ways than one. Today was one of those days. I've never considered myself to ever be capable of ending my own life but today proved to me that just about anybody is vulnerable, even those we consider to be the strongest amongst us.

I will remember Robert for who he was and what he had taught me. A man that stood by his principles and tried his best to help those around him. He found himself in a truly dark place and one he couldn't find his way out of. I hope that he has finally found the peace he was searching for.

Friday, October 5

Rostered day off.

Saturday, October 6

Rostered day off.

Sunday, October 7

Rostered day off.

Monday, October 8

Today, I returned to Thomson East and found the unit much the same as when I left it, minus two prisoners. As soon as I walked through the airlock, I was greeted by Thelma sitting in the station. Although we both attended the funeral, I hadn't heard from anyone over the previous weekend and thus hadn't had an update o the condition of David Bruce. If he had died, then our reports would be scrutinized on a whole new level as the case, us and our written word would be called to the Coroner's Court. Although I have never been myself, I have known plenty of officers that have, and none of them have had a good word to say of the experience.

Thankfully, David had survived his attack, although still in an induced coma. He had received a severely fractured skull, which had resulted in bleeding on the brain and the medics didn't know just how severe his injuries would be, once he woke up. Adrian had been placed into Murray North and was said to be in splendid spirits. It truly saddens me to know that prison, even the units considered punishment units, are seen as nothing but holiday camps by the prisoners housed in them. Currently, Adrian was suffering in a cell for one; a television including a dedicated movie channel; his meals brought to him three times a day; a complete shopping list including all the soft drinks, snacks and food he can afford; his laundry washed and dried by prison officers; an hour out in the sunshine; all the conversation he can handle with fellow prisoners in adjoining cells. It's definitely not the solitary confinement you might imagine.

Thelma finished updating me as Tom Grady comes walking through the airlock. We shake as he enters the station and update him on the fight we saw. Tom had been on leave for the previous week and hadn't been updated on any of the happenings from the previous few days.

Control calls for count and Thelma and Tom grab the muster sheet and begin their rounds of the cells as I fire up the computer and the kettle. It's all pretty much routine as they drop traps and counts heads, eventually returning to the station to tally their numbers. Once they agree on the total, Thelma calls it into control and we wait for the confirmation.

A short time later, Control calls count correct and Tom and I unlock the unit for another day. Once we finish, I return to the station as crooks begin to line up for the medical trolley that is already making its way through the airlock. The unit is the closest to the medical wing and thus benefits from being the first unit it visits.

The crooks line up and everything begins smoothly. That is until the nurse holds up her hand to a prisoner who's forgotten his ID card. Before anyone has a chance to move, he smashes his fist into the reinforced glass and the sound is not only spectacularly loud inside the tiny airlock, but also very defined as to what else has just occurred. The crook's face goes from a dark fiery rage to a ghostly white in less than a second as he looks at his hand. His legs look shaky beneath him before giving out entirely as he crumples to the floor, clutching his right hand by the wrist, tears of pain welling up. There's a roar of laughter from the other prisoners as I call a code Mike, watching as the crook stares at his hand with eyes as wide as dinner plates.

When we get the report back later, we find that Prisoner Lu has sustained a broken wrist, two broken fingers and a crushed knuckle. Two bone shards were protruding through his skin and a third was threatening to pierce through in another spot while his tiny pinkie was dislocated in two places. His entire hand required wiring and as we watch him wheeled out of the unit still nursing his arm, another crook summed up the thoughts of many.

"Over a fuckin pill. Gonna need more now, dickhead."

It was almost another hour before the unit was back to normal and the med trolley finally finished. Most crooks had gone back to their cells for whatever reason and Tom and I figured it was a good-a-time as any to do our cell searches. He pulled up the random list and much to our delight, found Lu's cell to be one of the three. We headed out and found the first two searches to be pretty much non-events with neither prisoner either complaining about the search or housing any contraband. But when we came to Lu's cell, we couldn't have been happier. Sometimes, on rare occasions, instinct plays more of a part than usual. The cell had a certain "feel" about it and although we found nothing to begin with, our persistence paid off.

I noticed quite a few body building magazines on the shelf above the toilet and during the first pass of the cell, didn't pay them too much attention. They weren't considered contraband and thus focused on the more usual hiding places. But then, once we finished our initial sweep, they came back into my eye and that's when I began to wonder. Lu was as skinny as a broom handle and never entered the gym area. He wasn't what you'd call the physical type and so the magazines looked out of place.

I grabbed the top one and flicked through, nothing appearing out of place. But when I grabbed one from the middle and flicked through, the story changed dramatically. By around a dozen or so pages in, a beautiful breast stared back at me, followed by another and then the unmistakable view of a carefully manicured pubic bush trimmed into a landing strip. Hidden amongst the pages of the body building magazines was an endless supply of pornographic images that had been torn from differing magazines. I grabbed another magazine from the middle of the deck and found numerous lesbian-themed pages, whilst another magazine had gay male porn in it. Pages and pages filled with every porn style you can imagine were contained within the magazine covers.

Tom had been inspecting the bed and was now lying underneath it with a torch in hand when I heard him mutter something. As he shuffled back out from under the bed, I saw something black and rectangular-shaped clutched in his hand. When he got to his feet and showed me his treasure, I grinned, impressed with the find. It was an iPhone. A tiny circular magnet had been glued to it's rear and then had been hidden behind one of the metallic bed beams nearest the wall.

We headed back to the station after locking his cell and grabbed an evidence bag. Thelma had a wide grin as we showed her the find and once we completed our reports, phoned the Sup. I noticed a few crooks standing above the station, leaning on the hand rails as they watched from the second floor of the unit. There was a whisper between them and I knew that we'd found something substantial, both items having significant value within a prison unit. When I looked up at them, they walked away, but not before mouthing something as they turned. 'Fuck' was the word I made out and I knew that they weren't happy. I wondered whether there would be repercussions for Lu once he returned from hospital.

The rest of the day went about quite normal and by the time we walked out, Lu still hadn't returned. The Sup said that he'd more than likely remain in the hospital for a couple of days which I thought was probably a good thing. I hoped that for his sake that the boys would calm a little by then and maybe the repercussions wouldn't be as severe.

Today was a good day.

Tuesday, October 9

Sick day off.

Wednesday, October 10

I was rostered in Admissions today and from the onset, knew it was going to be a good day. I knew this firstly because of the names I was working with, namely Daryl Foster, a fairly new officer that not only had a heart of gold, but also a very funny disposition. The second thing that ensured we were in for a good day was the list of moves for the day. Or should I say the *lack* of a list for the day.

The court moves consisted of just 6 crooks attending court, far less than the usual 30 to 40. Then there were 2 outgoing prisoners, a number normally between 20 and 30. Finally, the incomings were down to just 9 prisoners, and the prison they were coming from meant their arrival would be somewhere well into the afternoon. This left several hours of, well, nothing. It meant plenty of time to find a dark corner and chill or a bright corner to read a book. In any case, it meant for very little work.

By the time I arrived in Admissions, 5 of the 6 court attendees had already been processed. I helped with stripping the last one, then escorted him out and onto the court bus that was waiting out the back. Once he was securely seated in one of the on-board cells, I joined the rest of the crew for breakfast.

Morning count was non-existent for us as our cells stood empty. We waited for control to call muster correct and once they did, prepared for the two outgoing prisoners who showed up carrying their bags about 10 minutes later. Neither had very much property which meant a quick procession through each of the steps, namely property checks and a quick strip search. Once completed, each was sat in a cell to await their transport buses.

And that was it for the morning. While some people broke off to gather in small groups and talk shit for a couple of hours, I jumped on one of the computers and continued working on my book. There was enough time to get a few pages in and just as I was feeling the onset of hunger rumbles, was pleasantly surprised to see several trays carried past me and into the kitchen.

A function had been held in one of the front offices, some multicultural gathering for visiting dignitaries. There was quite a good deal of food leftover and much to the delight of myself and fellow officers, found several trays of cakes, pastries and elegant sandwiches waiting for our greedy fingers. There are two things officers enjoy above all else; a day off and free food. By the time I walked out of the kitchen, several Danishes and a good deal of sandwiches had been slaughtered by my hand, enough for me to contemplate loosening my belt.

And almost as if pre-planned, a code alpha was called for the hospital unit just as I sat back down at the computer. The run to the unit was not an easy one and I silently cursed every single treat I swallowed with each step. There were several other officers also running beside me and we heard the yelling as we reached the doors.

As we entered the unit, one officer was standing with a chair held out before him while a prisoner stood a few feet in front of him holding a mop out in front of himself. His face took on a look of defeat as he saw the number of officers now piling through the door and quickly dropped the mop, surrendering his hands before him which were subsequently cuffed. It turns out to be a minor difference of opinion between a nurse and a prisoner, with the officer caught in the middle. It's a pretty common occurrence, considering some of the differing attitudes that work within the prison environment.

I return to Admissions and resume my typing. Much to my enjoyment, the final transfers don't arrive until after I leave for home, the late shift taking over from us later that afternoon. I get a great many pages written and with no further codes or excitement, was able to complete two whole chapters.

Today was definitely a very good day.

Thursday, October 11

Rostered day off.

Friday, October 12

Rostered day off.

Saturday, October 13

As I have said in previous chapters, weekends have a completely different feel about them and once I head to Thomson East, am happy to see Tom and Scott Jones already in what looks to be a very deep conversation in the staff office. As I enter, they turn to me and share the news that will no doubt dominate that day's topics of conversation within the prison.

"Temple's gone," Tom says and for a moment, I don't catch on.

"Temple?" I ask and almost have a brain fart as I struggle to understand who they're talking about.

"The Gov," Tom adds and then the both of them just stare at me, waiting for my morning-brain to wake up. It suddenly hits me and they both nod as they see recognition wash across my face.

"Gone? How's he gone?" I ask as I stow my gear in one of the cupboards, then popping my lunch in the fridge.

"Apparently he got the tap on the shoulder yesterday afternoon. No-one is saying why but there's a whisper that he applied for another prison. Head office caught wind of it and, well, see ya later, alligator." John Temple had been the Governor of this prison for a number of years and although we never really interacted, seemed like an OK guy. Officers and management rarely mix so it's fair to say that I didn't really know the man. I do know that this was his first General Manager's role within a prison and am guessing he wanted to take on a prison of a different nature.

"Any idea which one he'd applied for?" I asked but they both shook their heads. I know from previous experience that the transition to a new Governor won't take long, the Deputy Manager taking the reins in the meantime.

We head for the station and once count is called correct, Scott and I head out and unlock the cells. During our trap count, I did notice that Lu still hadn't returned to the unit, his cell still locked and empty. That meant he was still in the hospital and expected back in the unit once fit enough.

The crooks exit their cells and begin the usual routine of breakfast, laundry and hovering around the station with the typical array of questions. The medical trolley enters shortly after and I catch up with Thelma who's the designated trolley escort. She spends the entire time telling me about some rescue kittens she's looking after and almost convinces me to take one. I resist, having several furred friends already and wave her off once meds are finished.

It's all pretty routine stuff and by the time lunchtime count is called, most crooks are already standing by their doors before the announcement is even made. The count doesn't take long to conduct and before long, everyone is eating a lunch of salad sandwiches. Like I've said before, a good day for us is a bad day for you and doesn't make for very interesting reading.

The day runs out fairly fast and although there is a minor altercation mid-afternoon, everything else is smooth sailing. The minor altercation was a prisoner called Jason Mills, who insisted on wearing his hat inside, a firm no-no considering the inability for the cameras to identify him. He was asked several times to remove his hat throughout the day and by the fifth time, Scott had had enough, confronting the prisoner and subsequently locking him into his cell, pending a warning and a Sup's hearing. Being locked up early is generally considered to be punishment enough, with most prisoners opting to learn from the experience and comply with directions. None of us could ever have foreseen the repercussions that would develop from this minor infraction but would definitely remember it for years to come when the rest of this episode played out in the coming days.

As we walk out after lockdown, the sun still partially visible over the horizon, we joke and laugh at the prospect of the end of another shift.

"When you back on?" I ask my off-siders as we head out into the carpark. Thelma is back the following day, while Scott won't be back until Wednesday. He tells me that he's taken leave tomorrow as his daughter is having her fifth birthday party and he'll be the official security officer of the jumping castle that's been hired. I laugh at the thought and clap him on the back as we part ways, each heading for our vehicles.

Today was a great day.

Sunday, October 14

Sundays are always seen as great days to work and although I was looking forward to another easy shift, found myself awoken through the night with severe stomach cramps. Although I won't go into the finer details of my nightly toilet stints, I can say that I didn't venture more than a few yards from the toilet bowl for the next day or so.

Without pun intended, today was a real crappy day.

Monday, October, 15

Rostered day off.

Tuesday, October 16

Rostered day off.

Wednesday, October 17

I was surprised to be back in Thomson East today, not because of the unit, but because I'd been in there a few times over the past week and am more accustomed to getting moved around. Having a variety of places to work in makes for a far more interesting day as opposed to sitting in the same unit day after day.

In any case, Scott Jones was already in the station when I entered the unit and I almost got to him before his face changed as he looked past me. I turned to see Tony Malone coming through the airlock and found all the enthusiasm drop to my feet. If you have been following my journeys through the different chapters of Prison Days, then you will already be aware of the day that lay ahead.

Scott and I shook and when Tony came to the station, offered him a handshake which he returned. I checked the unit muster and found that Lu still hadn't returned. A few other names had been replaced by new ones and the current number of prisoners housed within Thomson East had risen to 64.

While Tony and Scott made their way around the unit conducting count, I jumped on the computer and checked my emails. They tend to pile up quite quickly and if not handled at least once or twice a week, can begin to add up into 4 figure territory. There were the usual ones that didn't concern me, those that discussed daily moves, upcoming events and daily incident reports. The daily reports are of quite a significance as it gives you a run down of what happens in other units in case you are rostered in them. Good to be aware of any incidents that may impact future events.

When the boys return from their rounds, I managed to dwindle my emails down to under a hundred. One had been sent advising of the expected arrival of a new Governor in the coming days but failed to go into much detail. There was another that advised us that Lu would be moving units upon his return to the prison on Thursday the 18th. Due to expected repercussions, he was being moved into protection for the time being. Loddon North would be his home for the following few weeks and would be up to us to empty his cell today, moving his belongings to his new unit.

Count is called correct shortly after we call our number through and Tony and I head out to unlock everyone. By the time we return to the station, the unit is a hive of activity. Scott begins to answer prisoner's requests for various things such as Request Forms, toiletries, account balances and movement slips for various destinations. I grab a bag and head up to Lu's cell to begin the task of bagging his shit up. Although needing a couple of prods, Tony eventually grabs the cell clearance book and follows me to take note of each item, a requirement when clearing a cell for a prisoner that isn't present.

Thankfully, Lu's cell is one that's not nearly as full of property as some of the cells within the unit. Some prisoners can have as much as 3 or 4 large bags worth of items. Turns out Lu only has one. There isn't a lot of personal items considering the porn stack that he was selling or renting, but I figured he was probably being paid with drugs. Junkies rarely have a lot of personal items, more likely to sell things for a quick hit.

Once the cell is cleared of property and locked back up, I take the bag to the office, then call for a general duties officer to come and take it to the new unit. It doesn't take long before they show and the entire process is completed before 9 o'clock. As the GD heads out through the airlock, I check the list of random searches for the day, then take Tony to conduct them before he has a chance to get comfortable in his seat. His groan falls on deaf ears as I head to the first cell.

Out of the 3 cells we search, there is only a single cigarette to be found. I find it wrapped in plastic and hidden in a container of coffee. I call the prisoner to his cell and he admits ownership when I hold it up for him to see. The grin on his face tells me that he was expecting it and he doesn't complain when I confiscate his TV for 72 hours.

The day continues quietly until lunchtime count is called. The announcement is made and the prisoners begin to line up by their doors as the kitchen crew continue to prepare the meal that will be served once the muster is broken off. For once, Tony actually volunteers for something, grabbing the muster sheet and conducting the cell-to-cell count while Scott and I stand in the middle of the unit and conduct stationary counts from where we stood. As Tony passes by above me, I heard him speak to one of the prisoners as he's marking off names.

"Still no TV, Jason? Dam," he said in a gloating tone and I look up to see that the prisoner who he had spoken to was Jason Mills. I'd completely forgotten about the hat incident a few days prior and hadn't checked on the eventual outcome of the Sup's punishment. Turns out that the Sup was having a particularly stressed out day by the time he came to this unit to deal with Jason, taking his TV off him for an entire week. I look at Jason again and see the fury in his face as he stares at Tony, walking away from him as he continued the count.

Muster was called off ten minutes later and the crooks began to line up for their meals. It was a lunch that consisted of fried dim-sims and hot chips and although we were offered our own plates, politely declined. As they ate, I went to the unit log and flicked to the page where the notes were kept of Jason's meeting with the Sup. There was a brief paragraph written, stating that Jason had spat at the Sup when offered a simple reprimand, claiming to have been victimized. He was subsequently locked down that day and lost his TV for a week. It could have been worse, as spitting at an officer can be classed as assault.

I headed back to the station and asked Scott if he was aware of the incident.

"He didn't look too happy when Tony made the remark to him. Maybe he's holding a grudge," I said and Scott seemed to consider. He stood and began to walk out of the station.

"Fuck it, I'll just ask him," he said as he headed for the stairs leading to the upper tier. Shouting suddenly began from the kitchen and I headed there to see what was happening. Two crooks were arguing over who was going to do the washing and as I tried to call to them to settle down, heard a sudden yell from above me. Looking over my shoulder, I saw Jason standing over something. I couldn't see what it was due to the angle, but I noticed that Scott was nowhere to be seen. Jason was swinging something in a wide circle then brought it down in a sudden strike that sounded dull. There was a prisoner standing just behind Jason and he looked white as a sheet. I pressed the panic button on my radio as Tony stood and began to run to the stairs, yelling something into his own radio. In all honesty, I had never seen him move so fast and I sprinted for the stairs fearing the worst.

Half way up the stairs I saw my worst fears as Scott was lying in a pool of blood at Jason's feet who was still swinging something around. He brought whatever it was down on Scott's head, screaming at him to 'fucken die, cunt'. Tony had reached the top of the stairs and had grabbed a garbage bin. He held it out in front of him and charged at Jason. I never paused, running at the prick with all of my 110 kilos. I caught him around the middle as Tony tripped beside me, the bin falling to the floor. Jason first gasped as the wind was knocked out of him, then screamed as he tried to break free from me. Tony was up on his feet and was about to grab an arm when I yelled at him to get his cuffs out. He did and as I struggled with Jason, trying to get on top of him, I saw Scott violently shaking on the floor behind us, the blood pouring from his head. He looked like he was having a fit and it made me sick to my stomach. I was so charged full of adrenalin that I never felt extra hands join in holding Jason down as extra officers finally arrived.

I didn't hear the urgent call for medical help as I sat on top of Jason, dragging one arm behind him as another officer grabbed the other. I didn't hear the other officers call for the unit to be locked down as I grabbed Jason's cuffed arms and helped drag him to his feet. I didn't notice the officer pick the sock up, the pool ball nestled in its base as blood dripped from it, splattering on the floor beneath. I didn't see the officer upend the sock, catching the blood-stained number 8 in the palm of his hand as I watched the Tactical Officers escort Jason from the unit. My legs felt weak, my knees threatening to quit as I watched nurses frantically working on my friend. They had his shirt open and were performing CPR as the blood continued to pool beneath him from his smashed skull.

I could only think of his wife and daughter, going about their day totally oblivious to the fight for his life that their husband and father was currently waging. I cried. I felt the hopelessness of not being able to help him, myself questioning whether I should have stopped him from climbing those stairs. Through thick tears, I looked at Tony as he stood leaning against the wall.

"WHY THE FUCK WOULD YOU GLOAT TO JASON ABOUT HIS TV?" I screamed at him as arms suddenly pulled me back. I hadn't noticed myself taking several steps towards Tony. If I had been able to reach him, I probably would have lost my job right there. One of the officers grabbing me slipped in Scott's blood and we almost went over. But more hands grabbed us from behind and I felt myself dragged away as the nurses screamed for an ambulance. One had already been called, although I never saw it arrive.

I was escorted from the building and taken to the main staff room. There, I was handed a coffee and made to sit so I could settle down. I needed to calm myself, the anger so raw inside me. The Supervisor eventually came and saw me, offering for me to go home once I'd written my report. I'm not usually one to run home but in this instance, I felt that I needed to. It affected me in such a strong way that I was still shaking as I was trying to type my report almost two hours later.

By the time it was finished and emailed to the Sup, my nerves were beginning to calm a bit, my hands no longer shaking. The ambulance had left quite some time before and the word had come that Scott was riding the edge, his head caved in from the impact. The first swing of the pool ball had hit him square in the face, fracturing his eye socket. He was unconscious before he hit the ground, Jason repeatedly hitting him with his weapon until I tackled him away.

As I drove home almost an hour later, having never met his wife or child, I found that they were the only thing I could think of. I prayed that they still had their husband and father. In the coming days I would find out that Scott died on the operating table twice before being resuscitated and stabilized. He would remain in an induced coma for 3 weeks as the doctors debated about how much damage had been caused.

Jason was moved to another prison before the end of the day and eventually charged with a string of offences. He was already serving a ten-year sentence for armed robbery. At the time this book went to print, we are still waiting for the latest charges to be dealt with. I eventually met his wife and daughter during one of my many visits and together we shared our heartache.

Nobody ever said this job was easy. But some days you wonder whether it truly is worth it. Today was a fucking horrible day.

Thursday, October 18

Remained off work at the request of the Sup.

Friday, October 19

Remained off work at the request of the Sup. I also attended a counselling session which I found to be very helpful.

Saturday, October 20

Rostered day off.

Sunday, October 21

Rostered day off.

Monday, October 22

It's never easy returning to work after a traumatic event so I was relieved to be given a General Duties shift as I came in. It meant that I wouldn't be stuck in any one unit and would keep me busy for most of the day, having dedicated duties at certain times. I did head to the staff room initially to find out any information about Scott and Jason and found out Scott was still in a coma. I also found out that shortly after Lu had arrived in Loddon North the previous Thursday, two crooks had beaten him with a pool cue and before officers could intervene, had picked him up and thrown him off the second-floor walkaway, purposely dropping him head-first to the floor. Word had it that he'd snapped his spine on impact and was now in the same hospital as Scott.

I have no doubt that word would have been sent to the new unit to "fix him". My guess was that he had been tasked with keeping the phone safe for the controlling gang of the unit and once they saw him arc up and punch the window, blamed him for bringing his injury onto himself. Or, if Lu had in fact been feeling threatened by the gang, his punching of the window may have been him attempting to bail from the unit, something that happens much too often. In any case, the word is that he'll never walk again considering his spinal injuries.

My first duty once count was called correct was to accompany the medical trolley to a couple of the units. The nurse greets me with a cheery 'howdy-doo' and we head off towards Murray North. Because of the events in Thomson East, my duties will keep me away from that unit until I feel ready to return. Personally, I've never been one to back away from a situation but in this case, prefer to work elsewhere if the situation allows for it. If management requires me elsewhere then so be it.

The med run goes by quite quickly, each unit sending a second officer to assist with crowd control. A couple of prisoners forget to bring their ID cards but aren't too upset when we send them back to get them. Each unit we attend has a different feel when we enter but each prisoner takes their turn at the front of the line and takes their medicine. It's only during the final unit's line-up that we have a prisoner attempt to divert his pills. As he pretends to swallow them with a sip of water, he turns to the other officer to present his open mouth. The only issue he had was that when he palmed them, he was so slow that both the other officer and myself, as well as the nurse, all saw him slide the pills into his hand instead of his mouth.

We try not to make too big of a deal with it and get the crook to retake them, watching as he first holds the pills between his teeth, then swallow them with water. We all know that if they truly want to divert, there isn't a lot we can do as the prisoner simply heads straight back to their cell and sinks two fingers down their throat, effectively regurgitating the meds in almost complete form. It happens all the time and can not be helped. With harder drugs such as methadone and bupe, prisoners are required to wait a specific time before leaving the dispensing area to reduce the possibility of regurgitation but no doubt it still happens.

When the med run is finished, another officer bumps into me and asks whether I'd mind swapping into the Sally port. It's an area I've always been fond of and agree without hesitation. The Sally port is the perfect place to spend the day, as it has zero prisoner contact, is isolated from the rest of the prison and allows me to spend some time working on my books. It's almost a gift as far as I'm concerned and I don't waste a second getting my butt there.

The afternoon is one of relative peace and quiet as work is reduced to several truck s and busses entering and exiting the prison. It's almost two an hour, leaving plenty of time for me to write. The drivers are friendly as I process each vehicle and all wish me a good day as they exit. I've written about the duties within the Sally port in previous books so won't bore you with the mundane bits.

Today was a great day.

Tuesday, October 23

As soon as I entered the gates of the prison, I knew something wasn't quite right. There were quite a few officers congregated in several groups and a couple of them were wearing medical face masks on top of their heads. The whole thing looked surreal, like something out of a movie. Turns out that 3 units had been confirmed as housing multiple flu victims. Medical staff were clear that infected prisoners needed to remain isolated. It was about the smartest thing I'd heard that morning.

I was asked to man the Sally port again and due to the outbreak, and the fact that I had children at home, was more than happy to oblige. The problem with infected prisoners who would be isolated in their cells, was that they still needed basic attention. Someone would still need to attend their cells with food and if an entire unit was locked down, there would be a ton of things to do.

It was quite a cool day and I put on my jacket as I entered the Sally port. With the wind blowing through the mesh doors with quite a bit of oomph, it can be considerably colder than outside. There's already a truck waiting to processed and I quickly stow my gear and signal the control room officer to raise the door. It's a vending machine supply truck and I go through the motions of checking it for any hidden contraband. I climb into the back, search the multiple boxes and also check the cabin of the vehicle. I also place the heartbeat monitor on the truck and let it run its check while I process the driver by scanning him for anything metallic. He checks out and a minute or so later, the monitor beeps its 'OK" signal. I gesture to the control room and they open the inner door. As the truck drives out of the Sally port, I hear another pull up at the outer door behind me.

The process repeats itself many times over, with mid-week being the busiest. There are Supply trucks, linen trucks, food trucks, prisoner buses as well as our own escort vehicles that make regular trips to hospitals and other daytrips. Prisoners could have a number of differing reasons to leave the prison including funerals, specialty appointments or specific transfers.

By 10.30, most of the traffic has cleared and I can finally focus on something else. I turn on the computer and check my emails, deleting them as I go. Once done, I open a fresh page and begin working on a new chapter of a fictional story I'm writing. It's called The Final Alibi and I have high hopes for it. Not only will it be my first fictional story, but it will also include quite a bit of the story being played out in a maximum-security facility.

I'm almost 500 words in when the inner Sally port door begins to raise. When it's high enough, I see the Duty Supervisor escorting four prisoners towards me, each carrying their property in clear plastic bags. I can tell from their faces that they are keen to get to the other side of the door behind me.

When they are securely inside the Sally port and the door is lowered again, I conduct a security check on each prisoner. Only once they confirm their ID's do I OK the control room to open the outer door. Unlike previous occasions, there are no police waiting outside; all the prisoners now walking back out into freedom.

As soon as they are gone, I return to my writing and manage another 1000 or so words before I'm interrupted again. Several tradesmen are entering the prison for some maintenance works and I need to not only process each person, but also individually itemize their tools with the tools-register. Things can go south very quickly if a prisoner managed to get hold of a screwdriver, power drill or worse. It takes almost 30 minutes to process the 6 men and their equipment.

By the afternoon, traffic begins to pick up again around 3 as several buses containing transfers arrive. By 5, there's a decent line of regular traffic coming and going and there's virtually no time for writing. My shift ends just after 6 as I'm relieved by a nightshift officer.

Today was a fantastic day.

Wednesday, October 24

Rostered day off.

Thursday, October 25

Although I had the rest of the week off (yes, four rostered days off. Have I mentioned how much I love the roster?), I decided to make myself available for overtime. I had nothing else planned and aside from writing, would only spend the day sitting around home. I figured that earning a bit of extra coin might ease the stresses of day to day bills.

The call came almost an hour before I was required so was in a mad rush to get ready and into the car on time. Traffic was hectic and I only just made it inside on time. I was given a shift in the Visits Centre and would normally be placed in the back of the building to conduct strips. But the back was already fully manned so I had the interesting task of escorting visitors from the Reception Centre to the Visits Centre. Thankfully, some days can be quieter than others and when I see the list, am happy to read that there are only 34 visits booked for the entire day. There's a huge gap in the middle due to the weekly training schedule. Each Thursday, for a period of 3 hours, the entire prison is locked down so staff can attend various training courses to stay up-to-date with qualifications. These training schedules can be anything from First Aid to X-Ray training. Most of these qualifications only last 12 months and thus require staff to be requalified.

I check the training schedule but already know the answer before I even open the attachment. My name won't be on the list as I'm on overtime, hence would not have been rostered. The roster is the reason the lockdown training days happen weekly. It's to allow all staff to attend, despite their varying roster requirements.

Because I was rostered in Visits, the start time is after count is called correct. It's also a much shorter shift than normal due to the Visits Centre being open for set hours each day. Visits officers work an entirely different shift to the rest of the prison so generally work more days each week to make up their 38 hours.

As I enter the front, I see Mavis Henderson and Sharon Ward sitting at the station. A third officer, Edward Ryan is just coming out from the toilet, clutching a newspaper in one hand. I do a quick walk around of the visits area, a requirement to ensure there's no hidden contraband anywhere before the visitors arrive.

When I enter the station, set up very differently to unit stations in that the entrance is behind a locked door. It's also a little higher than unit stations, giving whoever is sitting in it, a better viewpoint over the tables and chairs.

There's greetings all 'round as I shake with the other officers and when Mavis offers me the list, I say that I've already seen it. The three of them will man the main station, while three other officers will man the back. Once enough visitors have been processed out at the Reception building, I will make my way back and escort the groups here, ready for their family or friends. Just as I'm wondering how long it will take for the first group to be ready, the phone rings and Sharon gives me a thumbs up.

As I enter the rear Reception door, there's a group of around 10 visitors waiting for me. They all seem happy, some of them talking quite animatedly. I also notice a couple of people looking quite nervous, clearly their first time behind the walls. I try and make small talk with them as we walk up the long corridor and one of the ladies tells me about her visit. She is a Mum of a young 18-year-old that was done for speeding. Apparently, he was caught driving at 188km/h in an 80km/h zone. His main mistake was not pulling up straight away, instead trying to run. This meant he added an "evading police" charge which ultimately landed him in prison. I asked if she knew what unit he was in and when she said Thomson East, thought back to the attack on Scott.

The harsh reality is that most times, crimes and age are completely irrelevant when being placed into a unit. For the most part, it's more based on who the unit already houses. I can not imagine how frightening it would be for an 18-year-old to end up in an adult prison, much less the pain and anguish his family must feel. The lady asks me whether it's a good unit and I lie, saving her a little extra and unwanted anguish.

We reach the Visits Centre and I hold the door open as people shuffle in and make their way to the station. The officers begin to allocate each prisoner's visitors a specific table number and I help some find their seats. Only once the visitors are seated, are the prisoners phoned up. This prevents too many prisoners hanging around the area, mainly as prisoners tend to be very impatient and we don't need a crook shouting for his visitor while others are trying to have some quality time.

Almost as soon as all the visitors are seated, the phone rings again and my journey repeats itself, each time escorting a mixture of both confident and nervous visitors. As I hold the door open a second time, I see prisoners already seated at some of the tables, people enjoying chocolate, chips and drinks. It looks like a regular picnic ground and before I have a chance to enter, Mavis gives me the signal to return to the Reception Centre once more.

The process is repeated many times throughout the day, sometimes escorting a single person. It's not only family and friends that come to visit, often lawyers coming to visit their clients. These types of visits aren't normally on the visitors list so the total number isn't really known until the end of the day. Today doesn't seem to be a major "Lawyer Day" as such, saving my legs a few miles here and there.

All in all, it's actually a pretty good day. Far from the major assault that occurred here a couple of months ago where several officers were left injured. I enjoy escorting the visitors back and forth and find the day coming to an end quite quickly. As I return the final visitor to Reception and head back to the Visits Centre, Mavis and Sharon pass me, thank me for the day and head out. The rest of the officers are still sitting around the station and once I grab my bag, we all walk out together.

Today was a really good day and an area I definitely want to work in again.

Friday, October 26

Rostered day off.

Saturday, October 27

Rostered day off.

Sunday, October 28

Rostered day off.

Monday, October 29

Today is the first of a couple of night shifts. I'm rostered in Murray North and when I walk through the doors, am greeted by a jovial bunch of day staff. There are six officers and all of them keen to go home. Two of them are going trap-to-trap conducting count while the other four are sitting in the station talking shit. I shake hands with each then anxiously check the unit muster. Night shifts can be a make or break shift based on who is housed here. One particular name I always check for is Cooper Shelley (see June edition), a serial pest and frantic masturbator.

"It's a pretty good list, man," Rob Guthrie says, seeing me checking. "Should have a quiet night."

"Just the way I like it," I reply, grabbing a chair and jumping on the computer. I check my emails while the boys and girls finish up and once count is called correct, am left alone with 40 prisoners. The unit is fairly quiet for the time being and I take advantage by starting some writing. I'm rostered in here for two nights and know just how bad it can get. I get no more than 50 words into my writing before things kick off.

"Jesse!" one prisoner up on the second-floor yells. "Jesse!" The other prisoner doesn't respond. It soon becomes clear why. "Hey, Jesse you dog. How was the snitching today?" Jesse Wright is a protection prisoner who was beaten up a couple of weeks ago. Word has it that he lagged on another prisoner who was diverting medication and swapping it for sexual favours. The lagging not only ended the diverting for the prisoner he lagged on but it also caused the prisoner who was handing out sexual favours to be moved into a management unit, effectively isolating him from everyone. It definitely didn't go down well, hence the bashing of Jesse Wright. "Jesseeee!" Pretty soon other prisoners join the first, each calling for the dog to answer, asking if he wanted to be "butt-fucked". Jesse didn't answer any of them.

The burning continued for no less than two hours of constant abuse; shouting that was amplified in the relatively small space. I tried to block it out and continued writing, occasionally pausing to look over the unit. I really only had one duty and that was to monitor the intercom and unless someone pressed it, left me to my own devices. Some officers choose to do nothing more than watch TV while others might read. For me, night time was the perfect opportunity to write, although it was a hell of a lot more perfect when the unit was quiet and everyone was either tucked into bed or just watching TV.

The intercom is fairly quiet, the first call occurring just after 10 when a diabetic asks for his meal which has been put aside for him. I go and find it then walk it to his cell, passing it through the trap. He thanks me and I return to the station to continue writing. The unit is almost completely quiet as the clock reads 1102pm and I heat my dinner in the staffroom microwave. It is spaghetti bolognaise, homemade by yours truly. I eat it while watching some late-night TV although the X-Files episode that's playing isn't one of my favourites.

By 2 in the morning, the unit is almost completely silent and I was quite absorbed in my writing. I nearly jumped out of my skin when the intercom chimed next to my head. As I check the cell number against the muster, I instantly know the reason for the call before I even speak to the occupant. The cell is B14, a second-floor cell on the left side, its occupant being Jesse Wright. Based on the information that I know, as well as the burning from earlier that night, I can almost guarantee that he will try and bail from the unit. And the best way to do that is to wait until everyone else is asleep and then claim to have some sort of pain that will require medical attention.

"Please state your emergency," I say into the microphone, then listen as Jesse breathes heavily into the speaker.

"Boss, I've got chest pains." His voice is hoarse, almost gravelly and I know that my hands are tied when it comes to my own choices of response. Because he's spoken into the intercom, the conversation is automatically recorded. He's also told me that he's having chest pains which means he could be suffering a heart attack. I'm not a doctor and as such am unable to determine whether he requires medical attention or not. And he may well be having a heart attack, but I know he's faking it. It really makes no difference to me to call a code on him and get him a nurse. It will mean all night staff will have to attend the unit, something Sups hate, especially when its known to be a false code but I refuse to jeopardize my job for the sake of a simple report that I will need to write.

The other thing that will happen is the other crooks will know what Jesse is planning, and when the nurse finds nothing wrong with him, will advise the Sup that he will be fine to remain in the unit. The crooks will have a field day with him and the burning will be twice as bad. All of this I already know as soon as the words drift out from the speaker. I decide to offer him a one-time out.

"I'll have to call a code, Jesse. You sure?" He hesitates, then answers as quietly as possible to ensure no one else hears him.

"I need a nurse."

"OK, hang tight," I answer back, then grab my radio and call the code mike. Control responds almost instantly and announces the code to the rest of the staff. The radio comes alive as people begin answering, including the medical team that will attend. I prepare for the influx of people, turn the lights on in the main area and return to the computer to begin typing the report.

As the first people begin to arrive, I point them up to the cell then finish my report. It's already printed and signed by the time the Sup arrives and I set it on top of the bench for him. The nurses arrive shortly after and head straight to the stairs. The cell is cracked and I wait at the station in case I need to activate something.

The scenario plays out exactly as I predicted. Before the nurses are even out from the cell, the other prisoners are already starting the burn.

"Look fellas, that fuckin dog is trying to bail," one shouts under his door. There's hysterical laughing from several other cells.

"JESSEE! RUN BUDDY!" another yells. The unit is now almost completely awake as shouts and heckling come from all corners. Some of the other officers are wearing cheesy grins themselves, knowing what is playing out. A few minutes later the nurses step out from the cell and the door is locked, Jesse remaining inside. The Sup comes to the station and grabs my report, his expression clearly telling me what I already know.

Five minutes later the unit is completely empty again, only myself and 40 crooks left to ride the storm that has awoken. The heckling is relentless and less than an hour later the intercom goes off again. It's Jesse once more and when I answer, tells me he's still having chest pains. This time however, my response changes as the nurses had already seen to him.

"Just have to ride it out till morning, man. There's nothing I can do." He doesn't respond and I break the connection as the other crooks continue burning. It goes on for almost another full hour before they start to tire from the yelling. By 4 that morning, the unit is again almost silent and I manage to return to my writing for another hour and a bit before prepping for breakfast.

Just after 5.30 I begin making the toast for the unit, 160 slices of bread being run through an industrial toaster. They are ready to be handed out by 6 and as the first of the day staff arrive, I begin going trap to trap, handing each prisoner a plate of toast and condiments.

By 7, the day staff have all turned up and I bid them farewell, tired from a long night and knowing that I will be back to do it all again in 12 short hours.

Tonight, was a good night.

Tuesday, October 30

I return to the unit a little before 7, most of the officers sitting in the station. A couple of new prisoners arrived during the day but for the most part, not much had changed. They had listened to Jesse getting burnt a few times but otherwise had a fairly quiet shift.

Once count is called correct and the day staff leave, I flick the TV on and start my night with a couple of episodes of Seinfeld while the crooks hold various conversations around the unit, each yelling to someone from under their doors. A lot of the conversations are far from intelligent and I turn the TV volume up to drown them out. Listening to one crook telling another how he gagged whilst feasting on some chick he picked up at a nightclub because of the stink was not something I really wanted to hear.

The evening played out much the same as the previous night. The intercom went off several times, mostly prisoners asking what movies were due to be shown on the dedicated movie channel. The diabetic called up for his meal around 9.30 and by 10 the unit had fallen silent. I found a Star Wars movie on one of the channels and found myself enjoying it until the final credits started scrolling just before midnight. The burning hadn't been too bad and I was surprised when Jesse called me up again, claiming to need a nurse.

"You know what happened last night, Jesse. I can only get a nurse up here by calling a code. You want that?" There was no answer. "Jesse, you want me to call a code?"

"No, it's alright." I cut the call and jumped on the computer, waiting for the desktop to load after putting in my details. The unit was almost completely silent and it was probably a good thing, because if it had of been as noisy as the previous night, I may never have heard the noise.

Just as I began to type away, I heard what I can only describe as a very quiet moan. It wasn't the kind of moan you'd associate with pleasure, rather one more closely tied to pain. It was an almost grunt and I paused my typing as I tried to listen for it. I heard it again, almost muffled and left the station to investigate. There were close to 50 doors in front of me and the noise could be coming from anyone of them.

I was walking along the bottom tier when I heard the noise again, somewhere from almost directly above me. I frowned a little as I saw Jesse's name on one of the doors up there. I quietly climbed the staircase, then tried to sneak along the top deck as I listened intently. I paused beside Jesse's door then heard the noise again. It was coming from the cell directly beside Jesse and when I looked at the name, saw Dylan Williams. He was one of the new arrivals from that day and when I quietly opened the trap, was hit with the dank and pungent smell of coppery blood.

The cell was completely dark and when I switched the light on, had to stifle a scream that was building in my own throat. Dylan was sitting up in bed, the white sheet completely drenched in blood. He'd sliced his throat with a piece of plastic from one of the disposable plates, the blood pouring through his fingers as he held his hand over the wound. There was a splatter on the opposite wall to him and I scrambled for my radio as he looked at me wide-eyed. I will never forget the look he had in his eyes, the raw fear in them one I had never seen before.

I called the code, yelling for urgent medical help as Jesse asked me something from under his door. I told him to shut-up, instead trying to focus on Dylan. He spoke to me, his voice sounding as scared as his eyes looked.

"I didn't know it would take so long to die, Boss," was what he whispered to me. He was crying, his eyes now filling with tears as he tried to stand, instead falling forward, blood still pouring from his wound. "I need help," I screamed into the radio and control called for an eta on medical. I couldn't open the cell as night staff aren't allowed to have cell keys. It's a requirement as no staff member is allowed to open a cell after hours without just cause. Due to the odd staff member having inappropriate relationships with crooks, as well as some staff smuggling contraband in for crooks, cell keys can not be held by staff manning units alone after hours.

As the first staff began to arrive, I asked for permission to crack the cell via my radio. The Sup on duty gave it and as soon as I had 3 other officers, had one of them open it. The second it was open, we rushed in and began to try and stop the bleeding. We all wore gloves for fear of disease and I held my hand over the wound as someone else searched for a towel to use as a tourniquet. The stench was so bad, not from the blood but from the fact that Dylan had soiled himself, not surprising considering what he had done.

The medical team came rushing in and took over from us shortly after. I was glad to have them arrive and happily made my way out from the stink of the cell. Dylan looked white as a ghost, the blood looking like a massacre on the bed, walls and floor of the cell as the nurses frantically worked on him. He passed out at some point and when he was finally stretchered from the unit, appeared to me to be dead.

But he didn't die, despite losing a vast amount of blood. Dylan was rushed to hospital by emergency ambulance and stabilized by the medical staff. His cell was secured and eventually cleaned by unit billets trained in blood management. For me, seeing the look in that prisoners' eyes is something that I can never forget. He arrived in the unit from a previous prison where he'd been raped by another inmate. Dylan was 23 years old and was in prison for the first time. His charge was attempted burglary but word was that it was an ex-girlfriend that accused him. I don't know how true that is but I do know that the shame of the rape almost cost him his life. I hope he can find the help he needs to get through it.

When I walk out a few hours later, I remember the look in his eyes, the fear that was burnt into them and head home still numb from the experience. It's not something I hope to ever see again but know that with the environment I work in, most likely will.

Today was not a good day.

Wednesday, October 31

Although I wasn't rostered tonight, I opted for overtime and was pleased to get the call just as I arrived home from my previous shift. It meant that I could get the sleep needed for another night shift. There was a spare spot in the control room and it's one area that I haven't worked very many times before. The role is one of support to the two night control staff that man the numerous cameras, the prison intercoms as well as the Sally port. There is virtually no traffic after lockdown apart from some late prison buses. The other traffic that may come through is a garbage truck throughout the night as well as any ambulances that might be required.

Jason and Jackie are the control room officers and we greet each other as they buzz me in. It's a secure room with access only allowed for specific people. Shortly after arriving, they begin the count, calling for it on the radio. The phone begins ringing instantly with 25 units all vying to get their count called in so everybody can go home. Jackie answers each call and adds the number to the spreadsheet. The process takes around 10 minutes and once the final call is received, the final tally is added up. Much to the dismay of the staff, someone has called in the wrong number. Jason announces an incorrect count and the process is repeated.

Unfortunately, staff are required to remain on duty until the count is correct, regardless of finishing times. The longer it takes, the longer you stay. Incorrect counts can take two differing paths. The first is if the count is short. If it's short it could mean that a prisoner is missing, possibly escaped. It's one of the biggest fears of any prison officer and is something most people try to correct as soon as possible. The other is if the count is over. This could be due to a unit officer failing to write someone out in the log book after leaving for somewhere else. They may not have conducted a proper count, instead relying on the log numbers.

In this case, the count was over by 1 meaning we had too many prisoners. Once the fresh numbers start being phoned in, it doesn't take long to find the culprit. Comparing first count numbers to second count numbers soon reveals the unit responsible. The Sup is sitting in the control room and as soon as count is called correct, phones Thomson East. Each officer on duty in that unit must now write a report for an incorrect count before they can go home. I know the feeling as I have been there before and it's not nice unable to leave on time.

The airlock outside the control room begins to fill as officers begin to drop their radios and keys back to us. I take each and return them to their allocated places. The radios I put into chargers, ready for the next shift. The airlock doesn't clear for almost 30 minutes with a couple of hundred staff all trying to exit at the same time. It's a tedious process but one that can't be changed. I work non-stop with the keys and radio and am glad once I see the last of them.

Jackie selects the movies from the schedule and inserts the first disc, Rambo 3, into the DVD player. We have a TV on as well and can watch the movie if we choose. We can also switch it to normal TV but Jason is happy to keep Sly on.

Once the airlock is cleared and the movie is on, Jason and Jackie begin to complete their own tasks. It is their responsibility to allocate the next day's keys to each officer, as well as update overall systems around the prison. They also answer the intercom calls from unmanned units which begin almost immediately once Rambo begins playing. It would seem that Sly isn't as popular with some of the younger crooks as they request something else. Their voices sound deflated when told that the DVD's are selected by management and must be played as per instructions. In the words of someone much wiser, it is what it is.

For me, it is the start of a night of nothing. There's no spare computer in the control room so writing is out of the question.

There's no activity in the Sally port until after 1 the next morning, leaving me with nothing to do except enjoy the movies. There is one thing that I have always enjoyed whilst working with experienced staff and that is the stories. The control room is one of those areas where rumours come to die and truth comes to fruition. They hear everything and am almost knocked for six when I hear them start to talk about Emma Porter. She was an officer from my own intake course. Not one that I ever really clicked with, but would often greet her when seeing her around the traps. Turns out she'd been suspended that day. Apparently Emma had been engaged in some very, how can I say this, extraordinary activities behind closed doors with an inmate. Some of her unit staff had suspected something was going on between her and a prisoner when he continuously hovered around her. Word has it that she worked a night shift not long ago and snuck back into the unit after everyone had left and actually entered his cell, remaining inside it for almost a full hour. Other prisoners had commented on hearing their activities from their own cells. I'm ashamed to say that unfortunately it happens quite often. Lonely women and men who crave the friendship of anyone and will give in to the advances from prisoners looking for mules. I'm glad she was caught and hope she doesn't return.

I'm almost thankful by the time the garbage truck shows up after midnight, happily leaving the control room to process the truck in. When he leaves about half an hour later, I return to the comfort of my chair and pray for morning as I settle in to watch Tom Cruise playing a German officer.

Day staff begin to arrive from 5 onwards and I help staff dish out keys and radios to each. A couple of early buses arrive just before 6 and I process them in, only to be relieved by the day staff as the last one leaves. All in all, it was a good night, with no codes and no painful crooks buzzing up every few minutes like they do some nights.

I'm happy to walk out with the sun coming up over the far horizon, tired from my 3 nights. I think back to the month that was and remember all the craziness that once again has made me realize just how unpredictable this job really is. I think back to the words of someone long ago, who told me that no two days were ever the same. No truer words have ever been spoken regarding this role.

Author's Note

Thank you once again for joining me on yet another ride through the dark halls of maximum-security. I hope that the events of this month have opened your eyes to the stark reality of this place. I know from what I hear and see on television, that prisons all across the world have very similar stories. And the supply of newer and crazier stories never seems to end.

I'm already working on the November edition of Prison Days and can share with you some of the things that you will read about. One officer will finally retire after more than 30 years in the job while another begins his journey in the harshest way possible, resulting in him donning the nickname "Shit-lips". One prisoner will attempt to commit suicide in a very public way while another will cause an entire unit to erupt.

As always, I am grateful for your continued Support and look forward to seeing you on my Facebook page @prisondaysauthor or my website at www.booksbysimonking.com.

I look forward to seeing you in the November edition, due out on December 1st.

Simon